The Magic Rock

KAHLA KIKER

ACKNOWLEGDMENTS

I express my deepest and sincerest gratitude for all the people in my life. Without you, my success would not be possible. To my family - you are my life.

ADVENTURES IN K WORLD

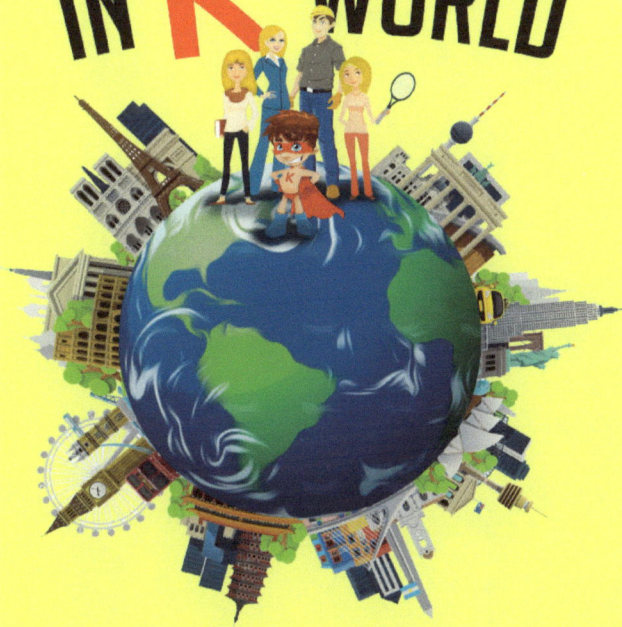

Meet the K Family!

Front: Kade a.k.a. Super K!

Back - left to right: Kiki, Mrs. K (mom), Mr. K (dad), Kat

THE MAGIC ROCK

K World is a place where all things in life are possible.

There lives a little boy named Kade who tries really hard to stay out of trouble. In K World, he is also known as Super K.

One day Super K was cleaning his room without being asked and found a rock with the letter K carved into it.

He was so excited that he ran to show his mom. "Mom! Look what I found! It has the same letter as my name!"

His mom replied, "Wow! Do you know what this means?"

"No, what?" asked Super K.

"It means you are doing something good without being asked," she said.

Confused, Super K asked, "But how did it get into my room?"

Then his mom explained that a magic rock appears when children are caught doing the right thing like cleaning their rooms without being asked.

Super K's mom also told him that once a magic rock appears, you get to put it under your pillow at night and make a wish.

When Super K heard that he would get to make a wish and it wasn't even his birthday, he jumped up and down and all around performing a happy dance.

That night at bedtime, he put the magic rock under his pillow.

Super K dropped down to his knees next to his bed to list his nightly reasons he had to be thankful and finished his prayer wishing for a new toy truck.

Then he climbed into bed.

The next morning, Super K awoke to a new toy truck lying next to his bed. He quickly looked under his pillow and *POOF!* the magic rock disappeared.

Super K jumped out of bed, grabbed his truck and ran into his sisters' room and showed them.

"Look! I got a wish and a truck for being good! The magic rock was real!" He shouted.

He danced around with his truck kicking his sisters' pillows around the floor.

Kat his biggest sister told him that he could be good again and pick up all the pillows he just kicked everywhere to which Super K replied, "I can't! It only works if you don't ask me, duh!" And he ran back out of their room.

Super K was full of joy that morning because he knew that as long as he continued to clean his room *without* being asked, there was a possibility that another magic rock would appear.

And that meant **ANOTHER WISH!**

ABOUT THE AUTHOR

Adventures in K World are a series of books written by Kahla Kiker and based mostly on actual events within the Kiker family. Without Super K, their lives would be incomplete!

ABOUT THE ILLUSTRATOR

Delores Sotelo has been drawing for as long as she can remember. Wanting to pursue her passion as a career, she is currently a college art student. She resides in Midland, TX with her husband, Daniel, along with their three cats and two dogs

www.ingramcontent.com/pod-product-compliance
Lightning Source LLC
Chambersburg PA
CBHW041240040426
42445CB00004B/99